My Mother's Language

La langue de ma mère

Abdellatif Laâbi

My Mother's Language
La langue de ma mère

Translated from French by
André Naffis-Sahely

poetry
translation
centre

First published in 2021
by the Poetry Translation Centre Ltd
The Albany, Douglas Way, London, SE8 4AG

www.poetrytranslation.org

Some of these translations first appeared in the chapbook *Poems*
(Enitharmon, 2008) and *Beyond The Barbed Wire: Selected Poems of
Abdellatif Laâbi* (Carcanet Press, 2016).

ISBN: 978-1-9161141-7-3

A catalogue record for this book is available from the British Library

Typeset in Minion by Poetry Translation Centre Ltd

Series Editor: Edward Doegar
Cover Design: Kit Humphrey
Printed in the UK by TJ Boos Limited

The PTC is supported using public funding by
Arts Council England

Contents

Introduction

Born in Fez in 1942, Abdellatif Laâbi was educated at the city's Franco-Muslim Lycée and began writing at age fourteen, the year Morocco achieved its independence from France. Initially intending to study philosophy and cinema, he instead enrolled in the faculty of literature at Mohammed V University in Rabat. While still a student, Laâbi co-founded the Moroccan University Theatre in 1963, where he first met Jocelyne Lecuelle, a French student whose family had emigrated from Lyon to Meknès in 1950 and who became Laâbi's wife in 1964. A year later, in March 1965, thousands of students and workers took to the streets of Casablanca to protest the rising cost of living, only to be murdered by the army, which had been called in by the country's tyrannical monarch, Hassan II, who went on to dissolve parliament and ordered the kidnapping and execution of Mehdi Ben Barka, a leading light of the anti-colonial movement. The exact details of Ben Barka's death are still unknown.

These were but the beginnings of the 'years of lead', a tumultuous time in Moroccan history that extended all the way into the 1990s, a period which saw hundreds of dissidents imprisoned, tortured, or 'disappeared', in a pattern resembling that of Latin America's 'dirty wars'. Radicalised by the horrors around him, Laâbi quickly became the embodiment of the engagé poet. In an interview published almost twenty years later, in 1985, Laâbi would say: 'I accept the term 'engaged poetry' when it… pursues its adventure to the end and does not fear being called to account or subjected to burning interrogations.' Laâbi's choice to write in French, the colonial *lingua franca*, rather than Arabic, should not be taken lightly. In numerous interviews, Laâbi has stressed that while he is now at peace with this decision, he remembers it as more of a necessity. Like countless others, Laâbi did not grow up in country where he was free to learn the language of his own people and as a result suffered from a linguistic anxiety that has affected nearly all of his coevals; an anxiety unfortunately typical to those raised with two or more languages, a master tongue and a slave tongue.

In 1966, Laâbi founded the magazine *Souffles* (*Breaths*), which helped launch the careers of writers such as Mohammed Khaïr-Eddine, Mostafa Nissaboury, Tahar Ben Jelloun and Abdelkebir Khatibi, who have since come to symbolise that period in time. *Souffles* left an indelible mark on North African literature. Influenced by Frantz Fanon, Aimé Césaire, Mário de Andrade and René Depestre, *Souffles* sought to transcend the coloniser/colonised dialectic, as well as challenge literary conventions and political dogmas. As Laâbi wrote in the first issue's editorial: 'Poetry is the only means left to man to proclaim his dignity, to be more than just a number, so that his breath will remain forever imprinted and attested to by his cry.' Radicalised by the Arab defeat in the Six-Day War of 1967, *Souffles* took an even sharper political direction when Laâbi met Abraham Serfaty in 1968 at a debate on the Palestinian question. Born into a Jewish family in Tangier, Serfaty was a mining engineer and radical activist, who was eventually dismissed from his post at the Ministry of Economy when he took part in a series of miners' strikes.

Despite the success of *Souffles*, Laâbi clearly believed literature simply wasn't enough. We get a feeling of how torn Laâbi must have felt when, at the end of his first novel, *L'Œil et la nuit* (*The Eye and the Night*), published in 1969, he asked: 'Now we are dead tired of the past… but who are we?' That same year, Laâbi joined the Parti pour la libération et du socialisme, but left the following year, in order to help set up Ila al-Amam (Forward). Unlike the urban guerilla tactics favoured by hard-left groups at the time, and despite its members living under assumed aliases, Ila al-Amam adhered to the tenets of non-violence and limited its actions to distributing pamphlets critical of the government. Nevertheless, both Laâbi and *Souffles* were headed for disaster.

Early in the morning on January 27 1972, Laâbi, whose wife was expecting Qods, their third child, was arrested at his home in Rabat. A number of teachers, students and intellectuals, including Serfaty, were also taken into custody. Laâbi himself was savagely tortured for four days, an experience he likened to a 'strange baptism' in his collection of political essays, *Les Rêves sont têtus* (*Dreams are Stubborn*). Just over a month later, and thanks to numerous demonstrations by Laâbi's pupils and colleagues, the poet was freed, allowing him to see his newborn daughter, before being taken back into custody on March 14 and transferred to Derb Moulay Chérif, Casablanca's notorious torture centre.

All these torments would eventually feed into Laâbi's second novel, *Le chemin des ordalies* (*The Path of Ordeals*), which was published in 1982. After a series of hunger strikes, one of which lasted for over thirty-two days, Laâbi was eventually granted a trial in August 1973 and sentenced to ten years of imprisonment for conspiracy against the state. In February 1974, by which time he had become prisoner number 18611, Laâbi was transferred to Kénitra, a city by the sea, also the site of a U.S. Navy base. During these prison years, Laâbi wrote a collection of poems dedicated to Jocelyne, his son Yacine and daughter Hind, *L'arbre de fer fleurit* (*The Iron Tree Blooms*) while in Casablanca in 1972; *Histoire des sept crucifies de l'espoir* (*The Story of Seven Crucifixions of Hope*) an account of seven militants who were put to death on August 27 1974; and *Chroniques de la citadelle d'exil* (*Chronicles of the Citadel of Exile*), a selection of letters penned in Kénitra in 1976.

Compounding their family's trauma, Jocelyne herself was detained by Moroccan authorities for five days in January 1975, an experience which partly inspired her memoir *Liqueur* d'aloès (*Aloe Brandy*), the second part of which directly deals with her experiences as a prisoner's wife. In 1978, after three years of petitioning for medical care, Laâbi was transferred to a prison hospital to be treated for ankylosing spondylitis, a condition that often results in osteoporosis, spinal fracture, inflammation of the eyes and paralysis. In the meantime, an international committee was set up to lobby European governments to exert their pressure on Morocco to secure Laâbi's release. Thanks in part to these efforts, Laâbi was freed on July 18 1980, when Hassan II amnestied a number of political prisoners. In 1985, five years after his release, Laâbi left Morocco for France, where he and Jocelyne took up residence in Créteil, in the Val-de-Marne near Paris, where the couple still resides, though they frequently return to Morocco.

Aside from his prolific work as a poet, editor and activist, Laâbi has also devoted his considerable gifts to the art of translation, introducing Francophone readers to the Palestinian writers Mahmoud Darwish, Ghassan Kanafani and Samih al-Qâsim, the Moroccan Abdallah Zrika, the Syrian Hanna Mina and the Iraqis Saadi Youssef and Abd al-Wahhab Al-Bayati. His anthologies of Palestinian (1990) and Moroccan poetry (2005) have been highly influential. In addition, he has also written an autobiography, *Le fond de la jarre* (*The Bottom of the Jar*), several plays and children's books. It was only thanks to the publication of Laâbi's two-volume *Œuvre poétique* (*Complete Poems*) that readers in France finally began to realise that Laâbi's work places him alongside Nâzim Hikmet or Pablo Neruda, recognition that led to Laâbi being awarded the Prix Goncourt de la Poésie in 2009 and the Grand Prix de la Francophonie de l'Académie Française in 2011, two of the most prestigious awards France bestows on its writers.

André Naffis-Sahely

Poems

La promenade

Ce matin
après une longue claustration
on m'a permis de faire la promenade
quinze minutes
dans un couloir terrain vague
jonché de débris de verre
et de boîtes de conserve rouillées
Un «fonctionnaire» gardait la grille
À l'autre bout de mon terrain de parcours
un autre
le fusil en bandoulière
Tout cela en l'honneur
d'un homme malade
épuisé par quinze jours de grève de la faim
Mais ça ne me fait plus rien
d'être regardé comme un fauve
ruminant de sombres cavales
et dont il faut se méfier du moindre geste anodin
Je sais même que ces hommes-là
veillant sur la direction de me pas
sont peut-être compatissants
ou au minimum indifférents
question de faim et trop de misère
Il y avait un soleil à faire perdre la tête
le ciel était bleu
je ne savais plus où donner de la tête en regardant là-haut
Alors j'ai fermé les yeux
et je me suis baigné la face et les mains

Walking the Yard

This morning
after a long time in the hole
they let me out
for a fifteen-minute walk
into an empty corridor
littered with rusty cans
and bits of broken glass
An 'official' guarded the gate
While another
stood at the other side
with a rifle slung over his shoulder
All this for the sake
of a sick man
drained by two weeks of hunger strikes
But being watched like a wild beast
as though I were some gloomy horse
whose mildest movement should be distrusted
doesn't affect me any more
I'm even aware that those men
eyeing my every step
might even be compassionate
or at least indifferent
it's all a question of hunger and misery
There was a crazy-bright sun
and the sky was so blue
when I looked up at it I didn't know where to turn my head
So I shut my eyes
and bathed my hands and my face

dans ces troublantes noces des éléments
puis mon cœur s'est mis à battre
à son rythme naturel
celui du cours régulier de l'espoir

in that unsettling marriage of elements
then my heart resumed
its regular rhythm
hope's harmonious flow

Le Spleen de Casablanca [extraits]

Dans le bruit d'une ville sans âme
j'apprends le dur métier du retour
Dans ma poche crevée
je n'ai que ta main
pour réchauffer la mienne
tant l'été se confond avec l'hiver
Où s'en est allé, dis-moi
le pays de notre jeunesse?

*

Ô comme les pays se ressemblent
et se ressemblent les exils
Tes pas ne sont pas de ces pas
qui laissent des traces sur le sable
Tu passes sans passer

*

Visage après visage
meurent les ans
Je cherche dans les yeux une lueur
un bourgeon dans les paroles
Et j'ai peur, très peur
de perdre encore un vieil ami

*

Ce gris matin est loyal
Je lui sais gré du spleen qu'il répand
de la douleur qu'il recueille

from *Casablanca Spleen*

Amid the noise of a soulless city
I learn the hard work of returning
Inside my torn pocket
in a summer cold as winter
only your hand
keeps mine warm
Tell me, where has the country
of our younger years gone?

*

O how all countries look alike
how exiles resemble one another
Your footprints aren't the sort of footprints
that leave any trace on the sand
you pass by without really passing by

*

Face after face
the years die
I search for a glimmer in everyone's eyes
for a flower to bloom from their words
And I'm scared, truly scared
of losing another old friend

*

This grey morning is honest
I'm grateful for the spleen it unleashes
how it's such a fine connoisseur

de la gerbe des doutes qu'il m'offre
en bon connaisseur

*

Si je sors
où irai-je?
Les trottoirs sont défoncés
Les arbres font pitié
Les immeubles cachent le ciel
Les voitures règnent
comme n'importe quel tyran
Les cafés sont réservés aux hommes
Les femmes, à raison
ont peur qu'on les regarde
Et puis
je n'ai de rendez-vous
avec personne

*

Je me sentirai perdu
à tout âge

*

Je ne suis pas ce nomade
qui cherche le puits
que le sédentaire a creusé
Je bois peu d'eau
et marche
à l'écart de la caravane

of the pain it collects
and the bouquet of doubts it has offered me

*

If I went out
where would I go?
The pavements are raw and rutted
The trees look pitiful
Skyscrapers obstruct the sky
Cars rule as absolutely
as any other tyrant
Cafés are open only to men
Women, quite rightly
are scared of being stared at
And besides
there is nobody
to visit

*

I will always feel lost
no matter how old

*

I'm not the kind of nomad
who goes looking for wells
dug by the sedentary ones
I drink very little
and steer clear
of the caravan

19

*

Le siècle prend fin
dit-on
Et cela me laisse indifférent
Quoique le suivant
ne me dise rien qui vaille

*

Dans la cité de ciment et de sel
ma grotte est en papier
J'ai une bonne provision de plumes
et de quoi faire du café
Mes idées n'ont pas d'ombre
pas plus d'odeur
Mon corps a disparu
Il n'y a plus que ma tête
dans cette grotte en papier

*

J'essaye de vivre
La tâche est ardue

*

Quel sens donner à ce voyage
Quelle autre langue
me faudra-t-il apprendre
Lequel de mes doigts
devrai-je sacrifier
Et si mes lèvres repoussent
saurai-je encore embrasser?

*

Soon this century will end
or so they say
And this leaves me cold
Although the next one
doesn't fill me with confidence

*

In the city of salt and cement
my cave's made of paper
I have a good stockpile of pens
and the means to brew coffee
My ideas cast no shadows
nor emanate any odours
My body has disappeared
and inside that paper cave
there is only my head

*

I'm trying to keep living
and the task is most arduous

*

What meaning shall I ascribe to this journey
Which other language
shall I have to learn
Which of my fingers
shall I have to sacrifice
And if my lips were to grow back
would I still know how to kiss?

*

Je frapperai
à toutes les portes de la ville
et je crierai:
Je suis étranger

*

Aujourd'hui
une étoile a dû naître
dans une galaxie
qu'on finira bien par découvrir
J'imagine la joie mauvaise
de cette garce
qui va survivre
à mes petits-enfants

*

Le froid
s'est installé
à la source

*

Pourquoi faut-il toujours que je relève
dans les mots, les gestes, les regards
la moindre imposture
et le subtil glissement
des civilités au cannibalisme?

*

Ah les yeux de l'homme
quand ils se trahissent

*

I will knock
on all the doors of this city
and scream:
I am a stranger

*

Today
a star must have formed
in some soon-to-be-
discovered galaxy
I can picture
that bitch's schadenfreude
at the fact she'll outlive
even my grandchildren

*

The cold
has set in
right at the root

*

Why must I always pick up
on the slightest duplicity
in people's words, gestures, looks
and the subtle slippage
from civility to cannibalism?

*

Ah the eyes of man
when they betray themselves

23

là devant vous
et se délectent
avec des grognements à peine étouffés
des vieilles histoires d'ogres et d'ogresses

*

Mère
je t'appelle
alors que tu n'es plus que poussière
Il faut que je te dise:
Je suis ton éternel enfant
Grandir
est au-dessus de mes forces

*

On rêve qu'on perd une dent
et l'on s'attend le lendemain
à l'annonce d'un deuil
Qu'y a-t-il de vrai dans cette superstition?
Peut-être simplement le signe
que quelque chose
va s'éteindre en nous

*

Poète
réjouis-toi de ces questions
qui te réveillent
au milieu de la nuit
et ne pâlissent pas à l'aube
avec les étoiles

*

right there in front of you
and delight
in the barely stifled grunts
of old tales of ogres and ogresses

*

I call out to you
Mother although
you're now nothing but dust
I must tell you:
I'll always be your perennial child
for growing up
is beyond me

*

We dream of losing a tooth
and the next day we wait
for someone's death to be announced
Is there any truth to that superstition?
Perhaps it's simply a sign
that something will be
extinguished within us

*

Poet
revel in all the questions
that wake you up
in the middle of the night
and do not vanish at dawn
with the stars

*

Cette nuit
je me suis encore réveillé
Nulle question ne s'est présentée
J'ai ouvert un livre
et c'est comme si j'avais ouvert
une antique blessure
Hé toi l'amoureux, m'écriai-je
comment peux-tu ainsi
te sentir seul au monde?

*

Pour retrouver le sommeil, je me raconte une histoire: Il
était une fois le fils de Shéhérazade. Il avait à peine six ans
et souffrait déjà d'insomnies qu'aucun médecin n'avait réussi
à soigner. Sur ce, un vieux sage, aveugle et un peu poète, se
présenta. Il ausculta longuement l'enfant et finit par confier à
la mère: «Chère madame, je ne voudrais pas vous manquer de
respect, mais ma conclusion est nette. Cessez de lui raconter
des histoires, et votre fils dormira de nouveau sur ses deux
oreilles.»

*

Les grandes feuilles m'intimident
Je les coupe en deux
pour écrire
des demi-poèmes

*

Les mots que j'aime
m'aiment-ils
Si je les égrène
que me restera-t-il à dire?

Tonight
I woke up again
No question presented itself
I opened a book
and it was as if I'd opened
an old wound
Hey lover-boy I screamed at
myself how can you think
yourself so alone in this world?

*

In order to go back to sleep, I tell myself a story: once upon a time, there lived Scheherazade and her sons. One of them was barely six years old and he already suffered from insomnia, which no physician had yet been able to cure. Thereupon a wise old man who was blind and a bit of a poet, presented himself. He examined the child at length and told his mother: 'Madam, with all due respect, my diagnosis is clear. Stop telling him stories and he'll sleep like a baby.'

*

Large sheets of paper frighten me
so I cut them in half
and write
half-poems

*

Do the words I love
love me back
And if I go through them one by one
what will I have left to say?

*

Verre après verre
nous réveillons la vie
Elle ouvre un œil
nous sourit vaguement
et se rendort

*

Quand le Mur
s'est écroulé là-bas
ce n'est qu'un ressort
qui s'est brisé
ici
dans le cœur

*

Ce que j'ai fait
je le dois à ma solitude
et à la solitude des autres
Mieux que la rencontre
il y a son attente

*

Je cherche la pureté
pour moi
et pour ce qui vient à moi
Je m'épuiserai un jour
mais je ne chercherai pas autre chose
que la pureté

*

Glass after glass
we wake life up
She opens an eye
smiles at us vaguely
and goes back to sleep

*

When the Wall
fell down there
it was but a spring
that broke
here
in my heart

*

All I have accomplished
I owe to my solitude
and the solitude of others
The expectation
is better than the encounter

*

I seek purity
for myself and
those who come to me
One day I shall wear myself out
but I'll never search for anything
other than purity

*

Le soleil est là
Je n'ai plus à l'acheter
Et bien vite je l'oublie
comme si j'étais fasciné
par les ténèbres

*

Les pays
maintenant
se valent
en férocité

*

Mon dieu
comme je me sens étranger
J'ai beau vouloir me mêler
à l'agitation du monde
je me retrouve à l'écart dans mon coin
Est-ce moi qui me punis
ou est-ce le monde?

*

Après les actes vains
les paroles vaines
donnant la nostalgie des actes

*

Les livres qui portent mon nom
et que je n'ose ouvrir

*

The sun's out and I
no longer have to pay to see it
And I quickly forget all about it
as if I was enthralled
by the darkness

*

Nations
are finally equal
now
in their ferocity

*

God
how I feel like a stranger
However much I wanted to throw
myself into the world's fray
I'm sidelined in my own corner of it
Am I punishing myself
or is it the world?

*

After vain actions
vain words
make one nostalgic for actions

*

The books that bear my name
and which I dare not open

de peur
qu'ils ne tombent en poussière
entre mes doigts

*

À force de côtoyer le monstre
l'odeur du monstre
te colle à la peau

*

Réveille-toi
rebelle
Le monde croule
sous les apparences
Il va crever
de résignation

*

Quand j'avais froid
et faim
(j'ai connu cela
ne vous en déplaise)
la vie m'était presque douce
et fécondes mes insomnies
Je pensais chaque nuit aux autres
(aux laissés-pour-compte
ne vous en déplaise)
et chaque matin
un soleil fraternel
venait me rendre visite

out of fear
that they'll crumble into dust
between my fingers

*

Rub shoulders with monsters
and your skin
will smell like monsters

*

Wake up
rebel
The world is collapsing
beneath the weight of appearances
It will die
out of resignation

*

When I was cold
and hungry
(believe it or not
I have experienced both)
life was almost sweet to me
and my bouts of insomnia fruitful
Every night I thought about other people
(meaning the marginalised
believe it or not)
and each morning
a fraternal sun
came to visit me

et déposait à mon chevet
deux ou trois
morceaux de sucre

*

J'ai besoin d'un répit
le temps que vous voudrez bien m'accorder
pour ouvrir une fenêtre
sur un temps que je n'ai pas encore visité
une île de chair princière
qui s'offrira à moi pour de bon
Je pousserai cette fenêtre bleue
et je ferai vite avant qu'elle ne se referme
Je ne dirai pas ce que j'aurai vu
Ce que j'aurai éprouvé
ira rejoindre le mystère
Si seulement vous m'accordiez ce répit
M'est avis que je vous rendrais
friands d'énigmes

*

Le poète invente une rose
mais ne sait quelle couleur lui donner
Comment est-ce la couleur du secret?
Tiédeur reconnaissable au creux de l'oreille
Visage rayonnant du père
emporté par la mort douce
Ride naissante au flanc de l'aimée?
Rien de cela ne définit une couleur

and left two
or three sugar cubes
by my bedside

*

I need a break
the time you might give me
to open a window
on a time I haven't yet visited
an island of princely flesh
that will offer itself up to me in earnest
I'll push that blue window open
and hurry before it shuts again
I won't tell you what I'll see
Whatever I will have proven or experienced
will go rejoin the great mystery
If only you'd give me a little respite
I'm certain I'd make you
fond of conundrums

*

The poet invents a rose
but doesn't know which colour it should be
What is the colour of secrets?
A familiar warmth in one's ear
A father's beaming face
carried off by sweet death
A budding wrinkle in your beloved's side?
None of this may be defined by colours

L'invention de notre poète
restera donc incomplète

*

J'avais une source
et j'étais économe de son eau
Je croyais fermement au partage
et ne pouvais soupçonner d'inconstance
ma source
Jusqu'au jour où elle s'est détournée de moi
prodiguant à d'autres ses bontés
Faut-il épuiser ce que l'on aime
afin de le garder?

*

Il paraît que la porte de l'enfer
avoisine celle du paradis
Le grand menuisier les a conçues
dans le même bois vulgaire
Le peintre manitou les a barbouillées
de la même couleur
Comment les distinguer dans cette pénombre?
Voyons
As-tu les clés
Quelle est la bonne
Et puis pourquoi te risquerais-tu
à ouvrir
ce qui ne pourrait donner
que sur le néant?

Our poet's invention will therefore
remain incomplete

                    *

I once had a spring
and I was prudent in using its water
I firmly believed in sharing
and did not suspect
my spring was fickle
Right up to the day it forsook me
and bestowed its bounty on others
Must we exhaust what we love
in order to keep it?

                    *

It seems the gates of hell
abut heaven's door
The great carpenter fashioned them
using the same vulgar wood
The supreme painter stained them
the same colour
How could you tell them apart in the penumbra?
Come on, take a look
Do you have the keys
Which is the right one
Moreover why would you risk
opening
what could only lead
onto nothingness?

La langue de ma mère

Je n'ai pas vu ma mère depuis vingt ans
Elle s'est laissée mourir de faim
On raconte qu'elle enlevait chaque matin
son foulard de tête
et frappait sept fois le sol
en maudissant le ciel et le Tyran
J'étais dans la caverne
là où le forçat lit dans les ombres
et peint sur les parois le bestiaire de l'avenir
Je n'ai pas vu ma mère depuis vingt ans
Elle m'a laissé un service à café chinois
dont les tasses se cassent une à une
sans que je les regrette tant elles sont laides
Mais je n'en aime que plus le café
Aujourd'hui, quand je suis seul
j'emprunte la voix de ma mère
ou plutôt c'est elle qui parle dans ma bouche
avec ses jurons, ses grossièretés et ses imprécations
le chapelet introuvable de ses diminutifs
toute l'espèce menacée de ses mots
Je n'ai pas vu ma mère depuis vingt ans
mais je suis le dernier homme
à parler encore sa langue

My Mother's Language

It's been twenty years since I last saw my mother
She starved herself to death
They say that each morning
she would pull off her headscarf
and strike the floor seven times
cursing the heavens and the Tyrant
I was in the cave
where convicts read in the dark
and painted the bestiary of the future on the walls
It's been twenty years since I last saw my mother
She left me a china coffee set
and though the cups have broken one by one
they were so ugly I never mourned their loss
even though coffee's the only drink I like
These days, when I'm alone
I start to sound like my mother
or rather, it's as if she were using my mouth
to voice her profanities, curses and gibberish
the lost prayer beads of her nicknames
all the endangered species of her sayings
It's been twenty years since I last saw my mother
but I am the last man
who still speaks her language

Les loups

J'entends les loups
Ils sont bien au chaud dans leurs maisons de campagne
Ils regardent goulûment la télévision
Pendant des heures, ils comptent à voix haute
les cadavres
et chantent à tue-tête des airs de réclame
Je vois les loups
Ils mangent à treize le gibier du jour
élisent à main levée le Judas de service
Pendant des heures, ils boivent un sang de village
encore jeune, peu fruité
à la robe défaite
le sang d'une terre où sommeillent des charniers
J'entends les loups
Ils éteignent à minuit
et violent légalement leurs femmes

The Wolves

I hear the wolves
nice and snug in their country homes
staring greedily at their televisions
counting bodies out loud for hours on end
howling at the top of their lungs
I see the wolves
without their sheep's clothing
eat fresh game at their thirteen-seater table
elect their token Judas by show of hands
drink the blood of a village
that is still young, a little fruity
the blood of a land strewn with mass graves
for hours on end
I hear the wolves
switch the lights off at midnight
and lawfully rape their wives

L'arbre à poèmes

Je suis l'arbre à poèmes. Les savants disent que j'appartiens à une espèce en voie de disparition. Mais personne ne s'en émeut alors que des campagnes ont été lancées récemment pour sauver le panda du Népal et l'éléphant d'Afrique.

Question d'intérêt, diront certains. Question de mémoire, dirai je. De temps en temps, la mémoire des hommes sature. Ils se délestent alors du plus encombrant, font de la place en prévision du nouveau dont ils sont si friands.

Aujourd'hui, la mode n'est plus aux vieilles essences. On invente des arbres qui poussent vite, se contentent de l'eau et du soleil qu'on leur mesure et font leur métier d'arbre en silence, sans état d'âme.

Je suis l'arbre à poèmes. On a bien essayé sur moi des manipulations, qui n'ont rien donné. Je suis réfractaire, maître de mes mutations. Je ne m'émeus pas à de simples changements de saison, d'époque. Les fruits que je donne ne sont jamais les mêmes. J'y mets tantôt du nectar, tantôt du fiel. Et quand je vois de loin un prédateur, je les truffe d'épines.

Parfois je me dis: Suis-je réellement un arbre? Et j'ai peur de me mettre à marcher, parler le triste langage de l'espèce menteuse, m'emparer d'une hache et m'abattre sur le tronc du plus faible de mes voisins. Alors je m'accroche de toutes mes forces à mes racines. Dans leurs veines infinies je remonte le cours de la parole jusqu'au cri primordial. Je défais l'écheveau des langues. J'attrape le bout du fil et je tire pour libérer la musique et la lumière. L'image se rend à moi. J'en fais les bourgeons qui me plaisent et donne rendez-vous aux fleurs. Tout cela nuitamment, avec la complicité des étoiles et des rares oiseaux qui ont choisi la liberté.

Je suis l'arbre à poèmes. Je me ris de l'éphémère et de l'éternel.

Je suis vivant.

The Poem Tree

I am the poem tree. Scientists say I belong to an endangered species, but nobody seems to care, despite the recent appeals launched to save the Red Panda and the African Elephant.

Some say it's a question of public interest, but I say it's a question of memory. From time to time, the memory of men reaches saturation point, when they offload the heavy weight of the past and make room to prepare for the beloved new.

These days, old species aren't fashionable. They have invented trees that grow quickly and make do with only water and sunshine, and who go about being trees both quietly and soullessly.

I am the poem tree. They have tried to manipulate me, but their efforts came to naught; I'm intractable, the master of my own mutations. Seasonal and epochal changes don't bother me. The fruits I bear are never the same. Sometimes I fill them with nectar, and other times with bile; and when I spy a predator from afar, I riddle him with thorns.

Sometimes I ask myself: am I really a tree? And I become afraid of walking, of speaking the sad language of this dishonest species, of grabbing hold of an axe and falling upon the trunk of one of my weakest neighbours. So I cling to my roots with all my strength. Inside their endless veins, I follow the stream of words right up to the primordial cry and break through the labyrinth of languages. I grasp the skein end and pull on it to free light and music. An image reveals itself to me. I produce buds that please me and look forward to the flowers. All this occurs under cover of night, with the help of the stars and rare birds that have chosen freedom.

I am the poem tree. I chuckle at all things ephemeral and eternal.

I am alive.

En vain j'émigre

J'émigre en vain
Dans chaque ville je bois le même café
et me résigne au visage fermé du serveur
Les rires de mes voisins de table
taraudent la musique du soir
Une femme passe pour la dernière fois
En vain j'émigre
et m'assure de mon éloignement
Dans chaque ciel je retrouve un croissant de lune
et le silence têtu des étoiles
Je parle en dormant
un mélange de langues
et de cris d'animaux
La chambre où je me réveille
est celle où je suis né
J'émigre en vain
Le secret des oiseaux m'échappe
comme celui de cet aimant
qui affole à chaque étape
ma valise

In Vain I Migrate

I migrate in vain
In every city I drink the same coffee
and resign myself to the waiter's impassive face
The laughter of nearby tables
disturbs the evening's music
A woman walks by for the last time
In vain I migrate
ensuring my own alienation
I find the same crescent moon in every sky
and the stubborn silence of the stars
In my sleep I speak
a medley of languages
and animal cries
The room where I wake
is the one I was born in
I migrate in vain
The secret of birds eludes me
as does my suitcase's magnet
which springs open
at each stage of the journey

Le soufi élégant

Quand le soufi découvrit le drap anglais, le cachemire et le foulard de soie, il déchira sa tunique de laine grossière: « Je me sentirai mieux dans ces étoffes, se dit-il. Elles donneront de la grâce à mes génuflexions. Je vais me couper cheveux et barbe, me brosser les dents trois fois par jour, utiliser comme déodorant une bonne eau de Cologne, jeter aux orties ma natte pourrie et la remplacer par un vrai tapis zemmour. Je me présenterai net et propre devant Dieu et m'est avis que mes prières gagneront en pureté. Dorénavant je ne vivrai plus d'aumônes. Je vais me trouver un travail honnête et d'un rapport honorable. Je me mêlerai à mes semblables, connaîtrai leurs soucis, apprendrai leurs blasphèmes, m'initierai à leurs amours terrestres, goûterai à leurs vins terrestres et peu à peu les ramènerai sur la voie du Mystère. Au fond, ma vie ne changera que de forme mais j'aurai inauguré une nouvelle voie mystique, celle des soufis élégants.»

The Elegant Sufi

When the Sufi discovered English wool, cashmere, and silk scarves, he tore off his coarse, woollen robe and said to himself: 'I'll feel more comfortable wearing these cloths. They will make my genuflections more graceful. I'm going to cut my hair and trim my beard, brush my teeth three times a day, use a good Eau de Cologne as a deodorant, chuck my tattered prayer mat away and replace it with a genuine Zemmour rug. I will show myself neat and tidy in front of God and I dare say my prayers will become purer. Henceforth, I will no longer live on alms. I'm going to find myself honest and honourable work. I will mingle among my kind, become acquainted with their preoccupations, find out about their blasphemies and initiate myself into the secrets of their terrestrial attachments, taste their earthly wines, and little by little lead them back to the path of the Mystery. After all, my life would only have changed in an outward way, but I will have paved a new path towards mysticism, that of the elegant Sufis.'

Le manuscrit

Je ne savais pas que Satan – Iblis pour les intimes – était de petite taille et qu'il était si indiscret, voleur de surcroît.

J'étais à mon bureau en train d'écrire quand il est venu s'asseoir en silence à mes côtés. Moi qui ne suis pas un géant, je le dépassais d'une tête. Je le détaillai donc avec assurance, relevai un à un ses signes distinctifs. De profil, son nez paraissait long. Son œil unique n'avait pas de cils. Une étoile à sept branches était tatouée à la commissure de ses lèvres.

L'ayant ainsi dévisagé et reconnu, je me suis remis sereinement à l'ouvrage. Tiens, un poème sur Iblis, me dis-je. Il a suffi que j'émette cette pensée pour que mon compagnon s'agite. J'ai vu une main très fine sortir de sa poche et se poser sur ma feuille. À chaque mot que j'écrivais il ajoutait un autre, avec un sens réel de l'à-propos je dois dire. Mais si l'une de ses trouvailles ne me plaisait pas et que je la raturais, il me rendait immédiatement la pareille.

Nous écrivîmes et corrigeâmes ainsi longtemps jusqu'au moment où la sonnerie du téléphone retentit. Je décrochai, attendis que mon interlocuteur se présente. Mais il n'y avait personne à l'autre bout du fil. Je finis par raccrocher avec rage.

Iblis avait mis à profit cet intermède pour disparaître, emportant avec lui notre manuscrit.

The Manuscript

I had no idea that Satan – or Iblis to his friends – was a midget, a gossip and a thief to boot.

I was writing at my desk when he came and sat beside me. I'm no giant, but I was a full head taller than him. I was easily able to look him over and make out his distinctive features one by one. In profile, his nose appeared to be long. His one eye had no lashes. A seven-pointed star was tattooed at the corner of his lips.

Having thus examined and recognised him, I returned calmly to work. Well, well, a poem about Iblis, I said to myself. The minute I had this thought my companion reacted. I watched a very slender hand emerge from his pocket and place itself on my sheet of paper. Whenever I wrote a word, he immediately added another – with what I must say was a real sense of appropriateness. But if I didn't like one of his ideas and deleted it, he immediately responded in kind to one of mine.

We wrote and edited for a long time until the phone began to ring. I picked it up and waited for someone to speak. But there was no one there. I slammed the phone down.

Iblis had taken advantage of this interlude to vanish, taking our manuscript along with him.

Il faut passer des nuits blanches

Il faut passer des nuits blanches, au moins quatre fois l'an.

Je ne trouve pas assez de fous autour de moi pour en faire davantage. Une nuit blanche, ça ne vaut rien quand on est seul. Elle exige le partage. Alors la ville s'offre sans penser à la mort. Les gargouilles font leur travail d'exorciste. Les muezzins se soûlent au coin des rues. Il y a toujours un couple qui se marie à l'aube, par tirage au sort. Le Chant des partisans devient une chanson à boire. Iblis se fait lyrique et distribue aux communiants des pommes rouges, non piégées. Les pieds foulent un trésor d'étoiles. Le sexe monte à la bouche comme le citron de l'huître.

Seuls les vagabonds peuvent être des poètes.

You Must Burn the Midnight Oil

You must burn the midnight oil at least four times a year.

There aren't enough crazy people around me to go further than that. A single sleepless night isn't worth much when you're on your own. It needs to be shared. Only then does the city open up to you without thoughts of death. Gargoyles carry out their work as exorcists. Muezzins get drunk on street corners. There is always a couple who get married at dawn by drawing lots. *The Partisans' Chant* turns into a drinking song. Satan starts to wax lyrical and hands out unbaited, red apples to the worshippers. Feet trample on a treasure-hoard of stars. The taste of sex rises in the mouth like lemon on oysters.

Only vagabonds can be poets.

La terre s'ouvre et t'accueille

À la mémoire de Tahar Djaout

La terre s'ouvre
et t'accueille
Pourquoi ces cris, ces larmes
ces prières
Qu'ont-ils perdu
Que cherchent-ils
ceux-là qui troublent
ta paix retrouvée?

La terre s'ouvre
et t'accueille
Maintenant
vouz allez vous parler sans témoins
Oh vous en avez des choses à vous raconter
et vous aurez l'éternité pour le faire
Les mots d'hier ternis par le tumulte
vont peu à peu se graver dans le silence

La terre s'ouvre
et t'accueille
Elle seule t'a désiré
sans que tu lui fasses des avances
Elle t'a attendu sans ruse de Pénélope
Sa patience ne fut que bonté
et c'est la bonté qui te ramène à elle

The Earth Opens and Welcomes You

i.m. Tahar Djaout

The earth opens
and welcomes you
Why these cries, these tears
these prayers
What have they lost
What are they looking for
those who disturb
your new-found peace?

The earth opens
and welcomes you
Now
you're going to speak without witnesses
Oh, you've plenty to tell
and have all eternity to do so
Yesterday's words tarnished by the tumult
will gradually burn in silence

The earth opens
and welcomes you
She alone desired you
without you making a move
She waited for you with none of Penelope's guile
Her patience was nothing but kindness
and it's kindness that brought you back to her

La terre s'ouvre
et t'accueille
Elle ne te demandera pas de comptes
sur tes amours éphémères
filles de l'errance
étoiles de chair conçues dans les yeux
fruits accordés du vaste verger de la vie
souveraines passions qui font soleil
au creux de la paume
au bout de la langue éperdue

La terre s'ouvre
et t'accueille
Tu es nu
Elle est encore plus nue que toi
Et vous êtes beaux
dans cette étreinte muette
où les mains savent se retenir
pour écarter la violence
où le papillon de l'âme
se détourne de ce semblant de lumière
pour aller en quête de sa source

La terre s'ouvre
et t'accueille
Ta bien-aimée retrouvera un jour
ton sourire légendaire
et le deuil prendra fin
Tes enfants grandiront
et liront sans gêne tes poèmes
Ton pays guérira comme par miracle

The earth opens
and welcomes you
She will not ask you to render accounts
of your fleeting affairs
wandering girls
heavenly bodies of flesh conceived in the eyes
fruits gifted by the vast orchards of life
sovereign passions that shine
in your palm's hollow
at the end of an indifferent language

The earth opens
and welcomes you
You're naked
And she's more naked than you
You're both beautiful
in that silent embrace
where hands can restrain themselves
and steer clear of violence
where the butterfly of the soul
avoids this semblance of light
to go in search of its origins

The earth opens
and welcomes you
One day, your beloved will rediscover
your legendary smile
and mourning will come to an end
Your children will grow
and read your poems free of fear
Your country will heal, as if by magic

lorsque les hommes épuisés par l'illusion
iront s'abreuver à la fontaine de ta bonté

Ô mon ami
dors bien
tu en as besoin
car tu as travaillé dur
en honnête homme
Avant de partir
tu as laissé ton bureau propre
bien rangé
Tu as éteint les lumières
et puis en sortant
tu as regardé le ciel
son bleu presque douloureux
Tu as lissé élégamment ta moustache
en te disant:
seuls les lâches
considèrent que la mort est une fin

Dors bien mon ami
Dors du sommeil du juste
Repose-toi
même de tes rêves
Laisse-nous porter un peu le fardeau

when men consumed by the illusion
will drink from the fountain of your kindness

O my friend
sleep well
you need it
because you worked hard
like an honourable man
Before you left
you left your office in order
neatly arranged
You switched off the lights
and on stepping out
you looked at the sky
which was almost painfully blue
You gracefully smoothed your mustache
and said to yourself:
only cowards
think that death is the end

Sleep well my friend
Sleep the sleep of the righteous
Rest well
from your dreams too
Let us shoulder the burden a little

Notes on the poems

'You Must Burn the Midnight Oil' – *The Partisan's Chant* refers to the Bolshevik song commemorating military victory in Russian Civil War.

'La terre s'ouvre et t'accueille' – Tahar Djaout: Ecrivain algérien assassiné en 1993 à Alger par des fanatiques. Texte écrit le jour de son enterrement.

'The Earth Opens and Welcomes You' – Tahar Djaout: Algerian writer killed in Algiers in 1993 by fanatics. The poem was written on the day of his burial.

Afterword

Mahmoud Darwish – a poet Abdellatif Laâbi himself translated into French – once asked the question 'what is it?' of poetry and then answered:

> It is speech, when heard or read,
> Of which we say: This is poetry!
> For which no proof is needed.

Laâbi's own work is unquestionably *this* poetry: raw, palpable, precise and, above all, futural in its undimmed suspicion of what is out there to be written in the first place. These are poems which most definitely outlive their conditions. His poetry is grounded on writing only that which is essential for the survival of the poem. His poems don't seek to coerce the reader into a singular reading, but prompt them to seek different routes within the poem. Moving between and across the past and the present, with an eye firmly fixated on a hoped-for future, Laâbi's poems articulate time as disparate junctures, poignantly summoning significant moments from his past containment, friendships and observations. With haunting lucidity, Laâbi's poetry re-engages temporalities to archive them, so as to reclaim – this time on his own terms – the time killed in the corners of his cell while in detention. In 'Walking the Yard' ('La promenade'), for example, varied temporal intervals are recalibrated – 'this morning,' 'after a long time in the hole,' 'for a fifteen-minute walk' – so the stasis of incarceration is reaffirmed but also memorialised in writing and therefore granted another cloth. Corporeally, the fragility of the body 'drained by two weeks of hunger strikes' is vividly juxtaposed with a vertical outlook to living as though to remind the reader of the visual body of the poem, upright and yet searing, traversing upwards, *contra* the horizontality of non-resistance. As Laâbi is aware, resistance, in Arabic, is premised on readjusting what is intrinsically bent. The sheer brilliance of the poem can be attributed to its observant movement which retraces life in walking without any noise, by lending an eye (and an ear) to observe only what is worthy of being seen and heard:

> So I shut my eyes
> and bathed my hands and my face
> in that unsettling marriage of elements
> then my heart resumed
> its regular rhythm
> hope's harmonious flow

The prisoner poet, like 'some gloomy horse / whose mildest movement should be distrusted' by his keepers, is once again in charge of his internal rhythms, or, as Henri Lefebvre suggests, is elevated to the status of a *rhythmanalyst* who 'calls on all his senses' and who 'thinks with his body, not in the abstract, but in lived temporality.' This is Laâbi at his best, shifting the gaze from the prisoner as a victim to that of an observant participant who not only 'sees back' but also privileges seeing as a mode of resistance through which the redundance of waiting is interrupted. Without blurring the prisoner-jailer dichotomy, Laâbi sees with his heart's eye and in so doing, he seeks alternative aesthetic routes through the body of the poem which mirrors, albeit in anticipation, his own body.

The dilemma of what *language* is has always been an existential quest of Laâbi's poetry, resulting at times in wedding some *Jahili* (pre-Islamic) Arabic poetics to the French. The most striking of all, in this regard, is the poetic engagement with the motif of *al-aṭlāl*, the ruins, literarily a recounting afresh of what is left behind. It was during his prison years that

Laâbi diligently and devotedly studied classical Arabic, stating in an interview that 'despite being a quest of mine for a long time, it was [then] when I found myself with too much time on my hands that I decided to delve deeply into Arabic'. This is not an ordinary statement but a position that has allowed Laâbi to engage two languages poetically in his writing. In his poem, 'My Mother's Language' ('La langue de ma mère'), Laâbi responds to language as both the written/uttered (corpus) and the body (corpse). From languages and dialects passed on from the mother to the son, bodies in the process end up swapping places. As the title states, it is through the possessive construct that a connection is forged between the mother and language and eventually between the mother and the son, like an umbilical cord that announces its presence through its past or more precisely through what is left of it in the first place. In the poem, time is anything but intact. From start to finish, the poem's task seems to retrace what can no longer be seen by the naked eye: it begins with the *mother* but concludes with *language,* thereby re-igniting a brighter bond that stretches generationally from the mother to the son through language. In assigning the mother what could be the only heritage/ inheritance that he is left with – language – Laâbi inverts his mother's non-presence into a *ṭalal* (ruin) to be returned to repeatedly.

Like a bare confession, 'My Mother's Language' pronounces language and the mother dead in different measures. The former – language – is to be resuscitated by being spoken by Laâbi himself while the other – the mother's body – is to be left to die in the son's absence. Rooted in a relation which pivots on collisional and yet complementary elements in heritage and inheritance, Laâbi swaps times with his mother. Eloquently relating the china cups he inherited from the mother to the ensuing fragility of time and what it brings with it, he returns once more to solitude as the overwhelming and only human condition.

Laâbi's clarity of expression should in no way mask the enormity of his thematics. What is at stake are the ways in which images in his work evolve or, more precisely, forge an afterlife beyond the narrative itself. Indeed, seeing Laâbi in English, a task which is sublimely made possible by Naffis-Sahely, is to recognise a continuum whose body is multiple and yet grounded in one inimitable soil that solely belongs to the poet. In this sense, what is intimate is equitably shared with the reader so the reader themself can enter the space alongside the poet without being led to think but to think as an equal.

In his prose-poem, 'The Poem Tree' ('L'arbre à poèmes'), it is the first-person singular that pervades his ode-like supplication to poetry. Contemplative and witty, while declaratively clear-cut, it inverts inwards so the reader can bear witness to the interiority that enables the speaker to be 'the master of my own mutations.' The poem tree is, of course, also the poet tree – the one whose itinerary is that of change. To corroborate its rootedness, the tree reverts to doubt as a questioning of what and who we are but not of our existence per se. It is, one might say, more a questioning of the self so fresher roots and perceptions are pondered in the process. The tree that bears ever-changing fruit is never content with the same poetic burden. It is a soul-searching tree for *the* poem: 'So I cling to my roots with all my strength. Inside their endless veins, I follow the stream of words right up to the primordial cry and break through the labyrinth of languages.'

The poem tree, according to Laâbi, is in constant search of confluences which traverse the poetic status quo – always on the lookout for an essence, a becoming. What might be seen as a semblance of a tale is now telling its own story. The tree which primordially is also the coffin, is the one that ushers in the new poem:

I am the poem tree. I chuckle at all things ephemeral and eternal.
I am alive.

Today, as I read and reread Laâbi, I return to a poet whose poetry has carved out paths which are neither monolithic nor monolingual but permanently in motion, where images and imageries are constantly bartered across and in languages. It is for this reason that Laâbi grants poetry free rein as if to say: it is through poetry that life is retained and can therefore be reimagined. As it is the poet-translator (or the translator-poet) who is writing, language always exceeds itself, persistently asserting its multiplicity – a multiplicity which is condensed and far-seeing, where immediacy is always at the forefront:

In my sleep I speak
a medley of languages
and animal cries

Yousif M. Qasmiyeh

Abdellatif Laâbi is a poet, novelist, playwright, translator and political activist. He is often described as Morocco's greatest living poet. Born in Fez, in 1942, Laâbi quickly established himself as one of the most prominent cultural voices of his generation. He founded the influential literary review *Souffles* (*Breaths*) which was banned in 1972 and led to Laâbi's arrest and imprisonment for 'crimes of opinion'. He spent eight and a half years in prison. Laâbi's most recent accolades include the Prix Goncourt de la Poésie for his *Œuvres complètes* (*Collected Poems*) in 2009 and the Académie Française's Grand Prix de la Francophonie in 2011. Laâbi's work has been widely translated and he has reciprocated, bringing some of the most important Arabic writers into French, including works by Mahmoud Darwish, Mohammed Al-Maghout, Saâdi Youssef, and Qassim Haddad.

André Naffis-Sahely is the author of the collection *The Promised Land: Poems from Itinerant Life* (Penguin, 2017) and the pamphlet *The Other Side of Nowhere* (Rough Trade Books, 2019). He is also the editor of *The Heart of a Stranger: An Anthology of Exile Literature* (Pushkin Press, 2020). He is from Abu Dhabi, but was born in Venice to an Iranian father and an Italian mother. He has translated over twenty titles of fiction, poetry and non-fiction, including works by Honoré de Balzac, Émile Zola, Abdellatif Laâbi, Tahar Ben Jelloun and Frankétienne.

Born and educated in Baddawi refugee camp in Lebanon, Yousif M. Qasmiyeh is a poet and translator whose doctoral research at the University of Oxford examines containment and the archive in 'refugee writing'. His poetry and prose have appeared in journals including *Modern Poetry in Translation*, *Stand*, *Critical Quarterly*, *GeoHumanities*, *Cambridge Literary Review* and *Humanities*. Yousif is the Creative Encounters Editor of the *Migration and Society* journal and his collection, *Writing the Camp* (Broken Sleep Books, 2021) is The Poetry Book Society's Recommendation for Spring 2021.

About the Poetry Translation Centre

Set up in 2004, the Poetry Translation Centre is the only UK organisation dedicated to translating, publishing and promoting contemporary poetry from Africa, Asia, the Middle East and Latin America. We introduce extraordinary poets from around the world to new audiences through books, online resources and bilingual events. We champion diversity and representation in the arts and forge enduring relations with diaspora communities in the UK. We explore the craft of translation through our long-running programme of workshops which are open to all.

The Poetry Translation Centre is based in London and is an Arts Council National Portfolio organisation. To find out more about us, including how you can support our work, please visit: www.poetrytranslation.org.

About the World Poet Series

The *World Poet Series* offers an introduction to some of the world's most exciting contemporary poets in an elegant pocket-sized format. The books are presented as bilingual editions, with the English and original-language text displayed side by side. They include specially commissioned translations and completing each book is an afterword essay by a UK-based poet, responding to the translations.